THE UNOFFICIAL HOGWARTS COOKBOOK FOR KIDS

50 MAGICALLY SIMPLE, SPELLBINDING RECIPES
FOR YOUNG WITCHES & WIZARDS

THE

UNOFFICIAL HOGWARTS COOKBOOK

FOR KIDS

ALANA AL-HATLANI

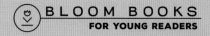

BLOOM BOOKS

FOR YOUNG READERS

Published by:
BLOOM BOOKS FOR YOUNG READERS,
an imprint of Ulysses Press
PO Box 3440
Berkeley, CA 94703
www.ulyssespress.com

ISBN: 978-1-64604-181-7
Library of Congress Control Number: 2021931310

Printed in China
10 9 8 7 6 5 4 3 2

Acquisitions editor: Claire Sielaff
Managing editor: Claire Chun
Editor: Renee Rutledge
Proofreader: Barbara Schultz
Front cover and interior design: David Hastings
Artwork: shutterstock.com except pages 17, 35, 40, 62, 83, 87, 89, 91, 107, 109, 114 © Alana Al-Hatlani
Production: Jake Flaherty

To magically minded young fans around the world

Contents

Introduction

Welcome, young witches, wizards, and non-magical folk alike! In the following pages you'll find magical, fantastical recipes inspired by what students might eat in the Great Hall at Hogwarts, plus some other meal ideas that witches and wizards in training might eat at other magic schools around the world. After all, there's only so much meat pie a kid can handle! It's important to fill your stomach with a variety of food groups while you're filling your mind with spells, potions, and facts about magical plants and creatures.

This book will provide some old British classics as well as some newer American favorites. You'll find the recipes organized by meal type, ranging from yummy breakfasts all the way to delicious drinks. If you are just starting out in the kitchen, you can begin with some of the recipes in the Snacks and Small Treats section, as well as in the Drinks section, and make sure to read through the helpful advice for beginner cooks.

Some of the more traditional dishes can get pretty fussy, so I've pared down the steps and ingredients to make the final product easier to achieve (especially if you don't have the help of a wand or self-stirring cauldron). That being said, the dishes you'll make with the help of this cookbook will certainly taste as magical as the ones from your favorite book series. Tuck in!

In the Home Kitchen

How to Cook without a Magic Wand

Advice for Beginners—Safety

Though this isn't potions class taught by an extremely strict professor, it's still very important to follow the kitchen rules. After all, you want to keep your eyebrows intact and avoid explosions or melting cauldrons. Take a look at the following safety advice before heading into the kitchen to brew up a potion or bake a magical treat.

- **Ask an adult before beginning:** Talk about what recipe you're planning to make; they might have some advice for you. Let them look over the ingredients and tools you'll need to make sure you're set up for success.

- **When in doubt, wash your hands:** Wash your hands before cooking, after handling raw meat, after cutting smelly ingredients like garlic, and after picking up something you dropped on the floor. Wash those hands!

- **Roll up your sleeves and pull back your hair:** Sleeves can get in the way and knock things over while you're cooking. They can also catch on fire if you're working over the stove. Be sure to roll your sleeves up so none of that happens.

- **Clean up after yourself:** Cooking can get messy, and that's okay! But it's important to clean up the mess after you've made it. Since you probably haven't mastered a room-cleaning charm yet, you're going to have to tidy up the old-fashioned way. You can even try cleaning as you cook so it isn't as big of a task at the end.

- **Ask for help before using a utensil for the first time.** Like I said before, you want to keep your eyebrows intact. Instead of barreling ahead, pause and make sure you're doing things correctly. Just as it's important to pronounce spells correctly, it's important to use tools in the correct manner.

- **Pay attention to hot surfaces.** Keep towels (both paper and cloth), oven mitts, and potholders away from the stove.

- **Do your homework!** Review the recipe directions and ingredient list before you begin to cook.

- **Prep all ingredients.** Take the time to gather and prepare your ingredients before you begin.

- **Practice knife safety:** Think "SASS."

  » Stop—Pause and make sure no one is within arm's reach

  » Away—Cut away from your body and fingers

  » Sharp—A dull knife is dangerous! A sharp, clean knife is a safe knife.

  » Store—When you're done with the knife, make sure to put it away in a sheath or knife block.

- **Another thing to keep in mind is to always cut on a cutting board.** Your parents won't be pleased if their countertops suddenly look like they've taken a beating by an enchanted and particularly violent willow tree.

- **Wear closed-toe shoes.** If you are just learning how to handle a knife it might be a good idea to wear closed-toe shoes in case the knife accidentally falls.

- **Turn off the stove.** If you're in the middle of cooking and you need to leave the kitchen for some reason, turn off the stove. You can turn it on again when you get back.

Common Recipe Terms

Al dente: Cooked until firm—not crunchy and not too soft.

Bake: To cook food in an oven using dry heat.

Baste: To add moisture to food while you're cooking it so it doesn't dry out.

Beat: To stir very fast until a mixture becomes smooth. You can do this with a spoon, whisk, or mixer.

Blanch: To boil fruit or veggies for a short amount of time to seal in color and flavor.

Boil: To cook in water that has reached 212°F.

Braise: To brown first, then simmer food over low heat in a small amount of liquid. The pan should be covered. This results in tender meat.

Broil: To cook on a rack under direct heat. You can do this in an oven.

Brown: To cook on high heat to add darker color to the food.

Caramelize: To heat sugar until it melts and turns into a syrup. The syrup can look golden, brown, or even dark brown.

Chop: To cut food into small pieces (think: the thickness of a pencil). If your recipe says "finely chopped," cut pieces to half the thickness of a pencil.

Cream: To beat ingredients together until smooth.

Cube: To cut food into pieces that are around ½-inch wide.

Dash: ⅛ teaspoon.

Dice: To cut food into very small pieces, around ⅛-inch wide. Sometimes dice and chop are used interchangeably, but in general, dice means smaller pieces than chop.

Dredge: To coat uncooked food in breadcrumbs, flour, or some other mixture.

Dust: To lightly cover a dessert with powdered sugar or to dust a surface or dough with flour before rolling.

Fold: To gently use a spatula to mix light ingredients (like beaten egg whites) into heavy ingredients. The point of folding is to try to keep as much air in the mixture as possible.

Glaze: To coat food in sauce, icing, or other glossy liquids.

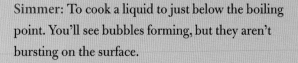

Grate: To rub food against a serrated tool, resulting in shredded bits.

Knead: To mix dough together using your hands or a mixer.

Mince: To cut ingredients into teeny tiny pieces.

Pinch: $\frac{1}{16}$ teaspoon.

Poach: To cook over low heat, with liquid just barely simmering.

Roast: To cook meat or veggies in dry heat in an oven.

Sauté: Also called pan fry, sauté means to cook food using a small amount of oil over high heat.

Shred: To cut food into narrow strips. You can use a knife or a grater to do this.

Simmer: To cook a liquid to just below the boiling point. You'll see bubbles forming, but they aren't bursting on the surface.

Slice: To cut ingredients into thin, similar-sized pieces.

Stew: To cook ingredients in liquid, usually in a covered pan on low heat.

To taste: To season a dish, usually with salt and pepper, until it tastes right to you. Not too salty and not too bland!

Whip: To incorporate air into a mixture using a whisk or a mixer.

Whisk: To incorporate air into a mixture, or to combine dry ingredients until smooth, using a fork or a whisk.

Zest: To grate the outer peel of a citrus fruit.

Breakfast

Rock Cakes

Rock cakes don't always have to be hard enough to break teeth despite what their name might suggest. Also called rock buns, these crumbly little cakes often feature dried fruit; but if you aren't a fan of raisins, try replacing those with the same amount of chocolate chips. These are best served fresh out of the oven (but be sure to let them cool just a bit) and with a cup of milk or freshly brewed tea.

Yield
6 cakes

Prep time
30 minutes

Cook time
15 to 18 minutes

2 cups flour, plus
more for dusting

2 tablespoons granulated sugar,
plus more for sprinkling

1 teaspoon kosher salt

1 tablespoon baking powder

½ cup (1 stick) unsalted butter,
chilled, cut into ½-inch cubes

¾ cup buttermilk

⅓ cup raisins

1 egg, lightly beaten

butter and jam, to serve

1. Preheat the oven to 400°F.
2. In a large bowl, whisk the flour, sugar, salt, and baking powder to combine.
3. Add the butter to the flour mixture and toss to coat.
4. Pinch and squish the cubes of butter between your fingers to break them into pea-sized pieces.
5. Add the buttermilk and raisins. Mix just to combine. The dough will be very shaggy.
6. Turn the mixture out onto a lightly floured surface.
7. Press the dough together to form a disk. Be careful not to knead the dough, but instead push and press it together, folding it over itself, until cohesive.
8. Roll the dough out to 1-inch thickness with a rolling pin.
9. Using a round cookie cutter, biscuit cutter, or the mouth of a drinking glass, punch out the cakes. Dip the cutter in flour every other cake to avoid sticking. Try to cut the cakes as close to each other as possible.
10. Gather any dough scraps back together into a disc, roll out to 1-inch thickness, and continue punching out the cakes. Repeat once more and then discard any leftover dough.
11. Place all the cakes on an ungreased cookie sheet, 1 inch apart.
12. Brush each cake with the beaten egg.
13. Sprinkle granulated sugar on top of each cake.
14. Bake until golden brown on top, 15 to 18 minutes.
15. Allow to cool on a cooling rack for 15 minutes before serving warm with butter and jam.

Bath Buns

Bath buns are a favorite of non-magical folk, especially in the UK, but our favorite groundskeeper was also known to serve these up at teatime. They are often sprinkled with crushed sugar or drizzled with icing, and some bakers even enclose a lump of sugar inside the buns for a sweet surprise. This recipe results in a delightfully airy bun, perfect to nibble on as a snack.

Yield
10 buns

Prep time
4 hours

Cook time
15 to 18 minutes

Dough
4 cups flour
⅓ cup granulated sugar
1 teaspoon kosher salt
1 teaspoon active dry yeast
1¼ cups whole milk, warm
zest of 1 orange
2 eggs, divided
6 tablespoons unsalted butter, cut into ½-inch cubes, room temperature
canola oil, for greasing

Topping
1 tablespoon whole milk
2 tablespoons powdered sugar
5 sugar cubes, lightly crushed
2 tablespoons caraway seeds (optional)

1. In a stand mixer fitted with a dough hook, combine the flour, sugar, and salt.
2. To a small bowl, add the yeast to the warm milk and stir to combine.
3. With the mixer on medium-low speed, add the milk to the flour mixture.
4. Next, add the orange zest and 1 egg. Mix for 8 to 10 minutes.
5. Slowly, one piece at a time, add the butter, until it's completely incorporated into the dough.
6. Scrape out the dough and form it into a ball. Place the dough in a greased bowl and cover with a damp cloth to rise for 2 hours. It should double in size.
7. Once the dough has doubled, turn the dough out onto a lightly floured surface.
8. Divide it into 10 equal pieces.
9. Roll each piece into a ball and place it on a parchment-lined baking sheet.
10. Cover the balls with a damp towel and allow to rise until doubled in size, 90 minutes.
11. Preheat the oven to 375°F.
12. Beat the remaining egg and brush it onto the buns.
13. Bake until the buns are golden brown, 15 to 18 minutes.
14. Allow the buns to cool to room temperature.
15. Mix the remaining 1 tablespoon of milk with the powdered sugar until smooth.
16. Brush the mixture on top of each bun, garnishing with the crushed sugar cubes. Sprinkle a pinch of caraway seeds on each bun, if using.
17. Let the icing dry, and then buns are ready to serve.

Crumpets

Crumpets are the perfect thing to have for breakfast, which is what many students and professors at the castle do. Our bespectacled hero even ate them on Christmas day during his first year. Melt some butter over your crumpets and enjoy them while they're hot!

Yield
12 large crumpets

Cook time
1 hour

1¼ cups flour
½ teaspoon kosher salt
⅔ cup water, warm
¾ cup whole milk, warm
1 teaspoon active dry yeast
2 teaspoons granulated sugar
½ teaspoon baking powder
nonstick cooking spray
butter and jam, to serve

1. Whisk the flour, salt, and warm water in a large bowl to combine.
2. Continue whisking the flour mixture for an additional 5 minutes, until the batter is smooth and air has been incorporated.
3. In a small bowl, combine the warm milk and yeast.
4. Whisk the yeast mixture into the flour mixture to combine.
5. Next, add the sugar and baking powder.
6. Let the mixture rest, covered, for 15 minutes in a warm place.
7. While the batter rests, prepare the cookie cutters. Spray the inside of each cookie cutter with nonstick spray. Then cut long strips of parchment to fit the inside of the cutters and line them.
8. Preheat the oven to 300°F.
9. When the batter has finished resting, grease a medium skillet with cooking spray and heat it over medium-low heat.
10. Start by placing the cookie cutters in the pan. Using a ladle, fill each cookie cutter up halfway.
11. Cook 5 to 8 minutes, until the tops of the crumpets have little bubbles across the surface and appear dry. A peak at the underside of the crumpets with a spatula should reveal golden-brown bottoms as well.
12. Use tongs to slide the ring off the crumpets, and using a spatula, flip the crumpets over to cook for an additional 1 to 2 minutes until lightly browned.
13. Remove the crumpets from the pan and place on a sheet pan. Place the sheet pan in the warm oven then repeat the process with the rest of the batter.
14. Serve warm with butter and jam.

Scrambled Eggs and Bacon

Here's a recipe for eggs and bacon, another breakfast staple at the castle. Though you can cook bacon on the stove like you do with eggs, I think it's easier to pop the bacon in the oven. Plus, you won't have to worry about hot oil splatter.

Yield

4 servings

Cook time

20 minutes

8 slices bacon

8 eggs

1 tablespoon unsalted butter

kosher salt and pepper, to taste

1. Preheat the oven to 400°F.

2. Line a baking sheet with aluminum foil.

3. Place the strips of bacon evenly spaced apart on the baking sheet.

4. Bake for 10 minutes and then flip the bacon slices over. Bake for an additional 10 minutes or until crispy.

5. Remove the bacon slices from the baking sheet and place on a paper towel–lined plate.

6. Next, crack the eggs into a medium bowl. Whisk together until no streaks of egg white remain.

7. Heat a medium skillet over medium-low heat and add the butter.

8. When the butter is melted, add the eggs.

9. Slowly stir the eggs using a wooden spoon or spatula, to scramble.

10. Continue stirring the eggs until set, about 2 minutes. No liquid egg should remain in the pan.

11. Season with salt and pepper to taste.

12. Serve the eggs hot with the bacon.

Porridge

A worldwide breakfast favorite, there's almost nothing more comforting than a bowl of warm porridge in the morning. Our brave trio ate this yummy dish throughout their years at school, as well as during visits to a certain ramshackle, family-filled home. Whether you've got a difficult potion to make, a transfiguration spell to work on, or broomstick practice, porridge will fill you up and give you the energy you need to take on the day!

<u>Yield</u>

4 servings

<u>Cook time</u>

15 minutes

<u>Porridge</u>

2 cups rolled oats

2½ cups whole milk

pinch of kosher salt

<u>Sweet Toppings</u>

1 green apple, diced

⅛ cup chopped
walnuts (optional)

4 tablespoons maple syrup

sprinkle of ground cinnamon

<u>Savory Toppings</u>

4 slices cooked bacon

¼ cup shredded cheddar cheese

1 scallion, thinly sliced

1. Combine the oats, milk, and salt in a small saucepan.
2. Cook over medium heat for 5 to 6 minutes, until the oats are soft and creamy.
3. Divide the porridge between four bowls and top with your favorite fruit, veggies, eggs, or cheese. Get creative!

VARIATIONS

For sweet porridge, sprinkle each bowl with the diced apples, walnuts, if using, 1 tablespoon of maple syrup, and a sprinkle of cinnamon. *For savory porridge*, crumble 1 bacon slice per bowl over the porridge, top with the cheese, and finish with a sprinkle of scallion.

Easy Marmalade and Toast

If you prefer toast for breakfast, here's the recipe for you! Marmalade is like a jam or jelly, and is usually made with oranges (although you're in charge of the cauldron, so feel free to experiment with other citrus fruits like lemon or grapefruit). It's even a flavor found in a box of every-flavor jellybeans. Since this recipe deals with boiling sugar, please be sure to ask an adult for help.

<u>Yield</u>

2 cups

<u>Cook time</u>

1½ hours

2 oranges, sliced in half
3 cups water
2 cups granulated sugar
4 slices bread, to serve
1 large piece of cheesecloth and butcher's twine

1. Squeeze the juice of the oranges into a bowl.
2. Using a spoon, scoop the flesh and seeds of the oranges into another bowl.
3. Thinly slice the peel into long pieces.
4. Fold the cheesecloth in half to create one thicker piece.
5. Place the orange flesh in the center of the cheesecloth and then gather it into a pouch. Secure with butcher's twine.
6. Place the juice, peel, and cheesecloth pouch into a medium saucepan. Pour in the water (the water should just barely cover all the ingredients; if it doesn't, add more).
7. Cook for 30 minutes over medium-low until the peels are tender and can be cut through with a spoon.
8. Turn off the heat and remove the pouch. Allow the pouch to cool to room temperature.
9. Once the pouch is cool, squeeze it into the pot to release all the juices.
10. Discard the pouch and then return the pot to high heat. Stir in the sugar and bring to a boil.
11. Reduce the heat to medium-low and cook for another 30 minutes. The mixture should be lightly bubbling.
12. Place a dish in the freezer while the marmalade cooks.

13. After 30 minutes, take a spoonful of the jam and put it on the plate. Wait 30 seconds, and then push a spoon through the mixture. If it wrinkles up, the marmalade is ready; if not, cook another 5 minutes and test again. Repeat the process until it does wrinkle.

14. Remove the marmalade from the heat and allow to cool to room temperature.

15. When the marmalade is at room temperature, place it in a jar with a lid to finish setting in the fridge.

16. Once cold, it is ready to use and can be stored in the fridge for up to a month.

17. To serve, toast the slices of bread and spread the marmalade on while still warm.

Banana Breakfast Potion

This smooth and sweet breakfast potion is inspired by a password the brave lions used to get into their dormitory tower: "banana fritters." Though instead of frying the bananas, they are will be blended into an energy-boosting potion. Be sure to use a powerful blending charm to get out all the chunks. If you don't have access to a wand, a non-magical blender or food processor will work just fine.

Yield

2 servings

Cook time

5 minutes

2 bananas, sliced into 1-inch pieces
1 cup frozen strawberries
¼ cup whole milk
1 tablespoon honey
2 tablespoons plain Greek yogurt

1. Add the bananas to a blender with all the other ingredients.
2. Blend on high for 1 minute until no chunks remain and the mixture is smooth.

Snacks and Small Treats

Caramel Apple Slices

Caramel apples are an iconic fall treat, so it's no wonder the students at the castle enjoy these around Halloween and during the Halloween feast (along with lots of candy, of course). This recipe is for caramel apple slices, which are much easier to eat than a whole, cumbersome caramel apple. Plus, they are extremely portable, which comes in handy when you suddenly have to evacuate dinner due to a troll in the dungeon!

<u>Yield</u>

2 servings

<u>Cook time</u>

10 minutes

1 green or red apple, cored, cut into 16 slices

16 caramel square candies or 1 cup chocolate chips

1 tablespoon heavy whipping cream

toppings of choice, like chocolate chips, sprinkles, or chopped nuts (optional)

16 toothpicks or lollipop sticks

1. Prep the apples by sticking one toothpick or lollipop stick into each slice.

2. Place the caramels or chocolate chips in a microwave-safe bowl. If using caramels, add 1 tablespoon of heavy whipping cream. Use 2 different bowls if you want to dip your apples in caramel and chocolate.

3. Melt in 30-second increments, stirring the mixture in between, until the caramels or chocolate chips are completely melted. Set aside.

4. Line a baking sheet with parchment paper.

5. Carefully, as the mixture will be hot, dip each slice halfway up in caramel and lay flat on the baking sheet to set.

6. Add the toppings, if using, while the caramel is still setting.

Cockroach Clusters

This recipe is inspired by the super-gross "candy" sold at the sweet shop in the village by the castle. But don't worry—there are no bugs to be found on this ingredients list! Creepy-crawly name aside, you'll be making a delicious, chocolaty treat.

Yield
8

Cook time
30 minutes

4 ounces semisweet chocolate, chopped
8 Nutter Butter sandwich cookies
24 pecan halves

1. Place the chocolate in a small microwave-safe bowl.
2. Melt the chocolate in the microwave in 30-second increments, stirring between each, until completely melted. Set aside to cool for 5 minutes.
3. Meanwhile, line a cookie sheet with wax paper or parchment paper.
4. Place one sandwich cookie on a fork and dip it into the chocolate. Flip the cookie over in the chocolate to coat both sides.
5. Lift the cookie out of the chocolate, tapping it against the edge of the bowl to remove excess chocolate, and place it on the cookie sheet.
6. While the chocolate is still wet, place two pecan halves end to end on top of the cookie. These are the cockroach shells!
7. Take another pecan half and carefully slice it in half to form two long pieces. Place these on the top of the cookie, hanging off slightly to form antennas.
8. Repeat with the remaining cookies.
9. Allow them to dry for an hour at room temperature or in the fridge until the chocolate is set, 10 minutes.

Chocolate Frogs

This recipe is surprisingly easy but results in realistic chocolate frog candies. Feel free to enchant your frogs after you're done making them, but be careful! Don't let them escape out of the train window.

Yield
12

Cook time
30 minutes

6 ounces semisweet
chocolate, chopped
12 gummy frog candies

1. Place the chocolate in a small, microwave-safe bowl.

2. Melt the chocolate in the microwave in 30-second increments, stirring between each, until it is completely melted. Set aside to cool for 5 minutes.

3. Meanwhile, line a cookie sheet with parchment paper.

4. Place 1 gummy frog on a fork and dip it into the chocolate, flipping it over to coat all sides.

5. Drain the excess chocolate off of the frog by scooping it up with the fork and shaking it gently. Hold it over the bowl for 30 seconds to let the excess drip off.

6. Place on the cookie sheet to dry and repeat with all the frog candies.

7. Allow to dry at room temperature for an hour or for 10 minutes in the fridge, until the chocolate is set.

Pepper Imp Bark

A delicious take on the classic wizarding treat, this peppermint bark recipe won't have you breathing fire or blowing smoke out of your nose, but it still packs a minty punch!

<u>Yield</u>

12 servings

<u>Cook time</u>

45 minutes

1 (12-ounce) bag semisweet chocolate chips

1 (12-ounce) bag white chocolate chips

1 teaspoon peppermint extract

12 crushed peppermint candies

1. Line a baking sheet with parchment paper.

2. Place the semisweet chocolate chips in a medium microwave-safe bowl.

3. Microwave in 30-second increments, stirring the chocolate between each until chocolate is completely melted.

4. Stir the peppermint extract into the melted chocolate

5. Pour the melted chocolate onto the sheet pan, smoothing it into an even, thin layer using an offset spatula or butter knife.

6. Place the chocolate in the fridge to set for 20 minutes.

7. Meanwhile, in another microwave-safe bowl, place the white chocolate chips. As with the semisweet chips, melt the chocolate down in 30-second increments in the microwave, stirring between each.

8. Remove the set semisweet chocolate from the fridge and pour the white chocolate over it, smoothing it evenly over the top with an offset spatula or butter knife.

9. Sprinkle the crushed peppermint candies evenly over the top and return the bark to the fridge to set for another 20 minutes.

10. Once set, peel the bark off the parchment paper and either cut into bite-size pieces or break apart into pieces with your hands.

11. Store the bark in an airtight container for up to 2 weeks.

Applesauce

Apple pie is a favorite dessert at the Great Hall feasts, but making pie can be pretty difficult even with the help of magic! Applesauce is a great way to get the flavor of that dessert but without all the fuss. Plus, applesauce is a perfect snack or side dish for any growing witch or wizard. Once you get the hang of this recipe, feel free to tweak it to your own taste (add more cinnamon, lemon, or sugar)!

Yield

4 servings

Cook time

20 minutes

4 Braeburn apples, peeled, cored, and cut into 1-inch pieces

1 cup water

⅓ cup brown sugar

1 tablespoon lemon juice

1 teaspoon ground cinnamon

pinch of kosher salt

1. Combine the apples with all the other ingredients in a medium pot.
2. Cook over medium heat for 20 minutes, stirring regularly and allowing the applesauce to gently bubble.
3. Once the apples are very soft, remove them from the heat and let them cool to room temperature.
4. When cool, blend the mixture in a blender or food processor until smooth.
5. Store in an airtight container in the fridge for up to a week.

Granola Bars "Owl Food"

Ever wonder what the owls eat up in the owlery at the castle? Here's my take on "owl food": delicious, homemade granola. Full of healthy oats and seeds, this snack will give you a great boost of energy (which will come in handy—you never know what things might come through in the mail).

Yield

8 bars

Cook time

20 minutes, plus 2 hours to chill

nonstick cooking spray

2 cups rolled oats

½ cup sliced almonds

¼ cup pecan pieces

¼ cup pumpkin seeds

¼ cup brown sugar, lightly packed

⅓ cup honey

4 tablespoons unsalted butter

½ teaspoon vanilla extract

½ teaspoon ground cinnamon

½ cup dried fruit of choice (optional)

1. Preheat the oven to 400°F.
2. Grease an 8 x 8-inch baking pan with cooking spray. Line the pan with parchment so that it comes up the sides of the pan and hangs slightly over the edge. This will help lift the bars out later.
3. In a large bowl, combine the oats, almonds, pecans, and pumpkin seeds.
4. Line a baking sheet with parchment paper. Spread out the oat mixture on the lined baking sheet.
5. Toast until lightly brown and fragrant, 8 to 10 minutes. Set aside to cool to room temperature.
6. Meanwhile, in a small, microwave-safe bowl, stir together the brown sugar, honey, and butter.
7. Microwave in 30-second increments until the brown sugar and butter have melted, 1 to 2 minutes.
8. Add the vanilla extract and cinnamon to the honey mixture.
9. Return the cooled oat mixture to the large bowl, add the honey mixture, and toss to coat evenly.
10. Add the dried fruit, if using.
11. Pour the mixture into the prepared 8 x 8-inch baking pan. Spread it evenly and then press it down firmly using the bottom of a measuring cup.
12. Chill for at least 2 hours in the fridge.
13. Slice the pan into 8 bars and serve at room temperature.
14. Store in an airtight container for up to a week or in the freezer for up to 3 months.

Fruit Skewer Wands

The castle serves up some pretty hearty dishes—so let's lighten things up with some easy and fun-to-make fruit skewer wands. These feature strawberries, which seem to be a favorite of the wizarding world, as they are not only served up plain for dessert, but also in dishes like strawberry trifle and strawberry ice cream (page 103).

<u>Yield</u>

6 skewers

<u>Prep time</u>

20 minutes, plus 30 minutes to chill

<u>Skewers</u>

12 strawberries, tops sliced off

12 blueberries

12 raspberries

2 mandarin oranges, divided into segments

12 red or green grapes

2 kiwis, sliced into half-moons

1 precut pineapple

<u>Yogurt Dipping Sauce</u>

½ cup plain Greek yogurt

2 tablespoons honey

1 tablespoon water

1 teaspoon vanilla extract

6 wood skewers

1. Assemble the skewers by adding one piece of each fruit at a time. Get creative with your patterns!

2. Repeat with remaining fruit and skewers.

3. Make the yogurt dipping sauce by whisking all of the ingredients together in a small bowl.

4. Chill the sauce for at least 30 minutes before serving.

Baked Sweet Potato Fries

A lot of snacks are catered to those with a sweet tooth, so here's a recipe for those who prefer something saltier. While the magical world serves up everything from mashed and boiled potatoes to roasted and jacket potatoes, my rendition—sweet potato fries—have great flavor and are super-colorful too! Serve these alongside any of the meals in the Lunch and Dinner sections, or enjoy them on their own.

Yield

4 servings

Cook time

40 minutes

2 sweet potatoes, peeled, trimmed on the ends, and sliced lengthwise then into ¼-inch-wide strips

3 tablespoons vegetable oil

2 teaspoons cornstarch

1 tablespoon chopped fresh rosemary

1 teaspoon kosher salt

½ teaspoon pepper

ketchup for dipping (optional)

1. Preheat the oven to 425°F.

2. Line a baking sheet with parchment paper.

3. In a large bowl, toss the sweet potatoes in the oil, cornstarch, rosemary, salt, and pepper, until evenly coated.

4. Spread the sweet potatoes in a single layer on the baking sheet.

5. Bake for 10 minutes, flip, then return to the oven for another 10 minutes, until crispy on the outside and soft in the middle.

6. Serve hot with ketchup, if using.

Lunch

Pumpkin Soup

There isn't too much mention of lunch at the castle in the books, though one can safely assume that pumpkin probably plays a role. After all, it seems to be a favorite of the magical community (pasties, juice, you name it). So here's a flavorful recipe for pumpkin soup—a great dish to have for lunch on a chilly fall or winter day.

Yield
4 servings

Cook time
30 minutes

2 tablespoons unsalted butter
1 large onion, roughly chopped
1 large carrot, roughly chopped
2 cloves garlic, minced
small bunch fresh sage
small bunch fresh thyme
3½ cups pumpkin puree
6½ cups chicken stock
⅓ cup heavy whipping cream
1 teaspoon kosher salt,
    plus more to taste
pepper, to taste
butcher's twine

1. Heat a large pot over medium heat. Add the butter and melt.
2. Once the butter is melted, add the onion, carrot, and garlic. Sauté until soft but not brown, 10 minutes.
3. Meanwhile, bundle the sage and thyme, together. Tie butcher's twine around them and add the bundle to the pot. This will make it easy to find and remove the stems later on.
4. Add the pumpkin puree and stock.
5. Reduce the heat to medium low and simmer gently for 20 minutes.
6. Remove the soup from the heat and let it cool for at least 20 minutes. Remove the bundle of herbs from the soup.
7. Blend the soup in a blender, working in small batches until all the soup is smooth.
8. Return the soup to the stove, heating it over medium-low heat.
9. Once it is simmering, add the cream. Cook for another 5 minutes.
10. Taste the soup and add salt and pepper to taste.
11. Serve hot.

Grilled Cheese

In between classes it's important to fill up with something tasty and satisfying. This recipe for grilled cheese goes well with the Pumpkin Soup (page 48) or the Magic Star Fruit Salad (page 63).

Yield

2 sandwiches

Cook time

10 minutes

4 tablespoons unsalted butter, soft
4 slices sandwich bread
4 slices cheddar cheese

1. Heat a medium sauté pan over medium-high heat.

2. Butter both sides of each slice of bread.

3. Place one slice of cheese on each slice of bread.

4. Sandwich two slices of bread together. Repeat with the other two slices.

5. Place the sandwiches side by side in the hot pan.

6. Cook until brown on the bottom side, 3 to 5 minutes, then flip using a spatula.

7. Press down on the sandwich with the back of the spatula to help melt the cheese. If the cheese isn't melting, adding a lid to the pan can help!

8. Cook until the other side is brown and the cheese melted, 3 minutes.

Green Salad

It's nice to pair any meal with a healthy side, which is why the matriarch of our favorite ginger-haired family served up a green salad to the crew before the World Cup. This version features a delicious homemade ranch dressing!

Yield
4 servings

Cook time
5 minutes

Salad
4 cups mixed greens

1 cup cherry tomatoes, sliced in half, or regular tomatoes, cut in wedges

½ large cucumber, thinly sliced

1 cup shredded carrots

Ranch Dressing
¼ cup sour cream

¼ cup mayonnaise

1 tablespoon lemon juice

2 tablespoons chopped fresh chives

½ teaspoon onion powder

½ teaspoon garlic powder

¼ teaspoon kosher salt

¼ teaspoon pepper

1. In a large bowl, toss together the mixed greens, tomatoes, cucumber, and carrot.
2. In a small bowl, whisk together the sour cream, mayonnaise, lemon juice, chives, onion powder, garlic powder, salt, and pepper to combine.
3. Add as much dressing as preferred to the large bowl with the salad mixture.
4. Toss to coat everything evenly in dressing.
5. Divide among four plates and serve.

Sheet Pan Pizza

This is a hands-on recipe for everyone's favorite food, pizza! Have some fun with the toppings by using colors that match your favorite house: yellow peppers and pepperoni for brave lions, green peppers or spinach for cunning snakes, yellow squash for loyal badgers, and chopped olives in the shape of a bird for clever eagles.

Yield
1 large pizza, 6 servings

Cook time
1 hour

Dough
5½ cups flour, plus more for dusting

2 teaspoons kosher salt

4½ teaspoons fast-acting or quick-rise yeast

2 cups water

6 tablespoons olive oil

Sauce
1 cup canned crushed tomatoes

1 clove garlic, minced

½ teaspoon dried oregano

¼ teaspoon kosher salt

¼ teaspoon pepper

To Assemble
3 tablespoons olive oil, divided

4 cups shredded low-moisture mozzarella cheese

3 cups assorted pizza toppings

1. Preheat the oven to 500°F.
2. In the bowl of a stand mixer fitted with a dough hook, mix 2 cups of flour with the salt and yeast.
3. Microwave the water until it reaches 120°F to 130°F.
4. Add the water to the flour mixture. Then add the olive oil. Mix to combine.
5. Slowly, on the lowest speed of the mixer, add the remaining 2½ cups of flour, ½ cup at a time until it's all incorporated.
6. Turn the dough out onto a lightly floured surface and knead the mixture for 1 to 2 minutes until smooth. Poke the dough with one finger; if it retracts back partially, it's ready to rest.
7. Rest the dough for 10 minutes, covered in plastic, in a warm place.
8. Meanwhile, stir together all the ingredients for the sauce in a small bowl.
9. Grease a rimmed baking sheet with 2 tablespoons of the olive oil, making sure to get all the way up the sides.
10. After the dough has rested for 10 minutes, lightly flour a clean surface. Using a rolling pin, roll the dough out to a rectangle shape roughly the same size as the sheet pan.
11. Gently pick up the dough and transfer to the greased sheet pan. If it's a little short, stretch it to the corner by gently tugging at the edges. If it's a little long, trim any overhang with scissors.
12. Using a large spoon, dollop sauce all over the pizza, leaving about a 1-inch border all the way around (this will become the crust). Use the back of the spoon to spread it evenly.
13. Next, sprinkle the cheese evenly across the pizza, avoiding the edges.

14. Now, scatter your remaining toppings on top of the cheese.

15. With the remaining tablespoon of olive oil and a pastry brush, brush the edges of the dough with the oil. This will create a nice brown crust.

16. Place the pizza in the oven for 15 to 17 minutes, until the edges are golden and the cheese is melted.

17. Let the pizza cool for 10 minutes before cutting and serving.

Dining Hall Club Sandwich

Our favorite trio and their fellow students had sandwiches for lunch (on self-refilling plates!) many times over the years, so here's an ingredient-packed take on what they might have munched on in the Great Hall.

Yield
4 sandwiches

Cook time
10 minutes

8 slices sandwich bread

2 large avocados, smashed to a paste

¼ cup mayonnaise

½ teaspoon garlic powder

pinch of kosher salt

4 leaves romaine, torn in half

12 slices turkey breast

4 slices swiss cheese

1 large tomato, sliced

8 slices bacon

1. Start by toasting the bread until light brown on an aluminum foiled–lined baking sheet under the broiler or in a toaster.

2. Add the smashed avocado, mayonnaise, garlic powder, and salt to a small bowl and stir to combine.

3. Spread the mixture evenly on all the slices of bread.

4. On four of the slices of bread, stack the lettuce, followed by the turkey, the cheese, the tomato, and finally, the bacon.

5. Top each stack with the remaining slices of bread and enjoy!

Witch Hat Quesadillas

The quesadilla is thought to have originated as far back as the 1500s in Mexico! Now it's a beloved dish all around the world, so I believe it should have its place as a lunchtime option for young witches, wizards, and non-magical kids alike. Add some extra magic to this dish by cutting the quesadilla into witch-hat shaped triangles. What you put in your quesadilla is up to you, but I recommend a good helping of cheese no matter what!

Yield
4 servings

Cook time
20 minutes

2 tablespoons canola oil, divided
¼ large onion, diced
½ pound mild chorizo
1 cup shredded cheddar cheese
1 cup shredded Monterey Jack cheese
8 medium flour tortillas
1 medium tomato, diced
½ cup sour cream
pickled jalapeños (optional)

1. In a medium sauté pan over medium heat, heat 1 tablespoon of canola oil.
2. Add the onion and cook until translucent but not brown, 5 minutes.
3. Crumble the chorizo into the pan. Cook until browned and crispy, 8 minutes.
4. Remove the chorizo mixture from the heat and place it onto a paper towel–lined plate to drain.
5. Meanwhile, in a small bowl combine both cheeses.
6. Heat another sauté pan over medium heat.
7. Add the remaining tablespoon of canola oil.
8. Place one tortilla in the pan. Sprinkle on ½ cup of the cheese mixture, followed by a quarter of the tomatoes and a quarter of the chorizo mixture. Press another tortilla on top.
9. Cook for 2 to 3 minutes, until the bottom tortilla is golden brown.
10. Flip and brown the other side. If the cheese is not quite melted, top the pan with a lid to finish melting it.
11. Remove the quesadilla from the heat and repeat the process with the remaining tortillas.
12. Cut each quesadilla into quarters and serve with a dollop of sour cream for dipping as well as pickled jalapeños, if using.

Mac and Cheese "Casserole"

Our wizarding world friends have a lot of casseroles at the castle, so I've taken inspiration from that mealtime staple for this recipe. Plus, everyone loves a boxed mac and cheese now and then, but there's something truly magical about a homemade bowl of gooey, cheesy goodness. This recipe makes several servings, so you can save your leftovers and eat them for future meals using a reheating charm or a microwave.

Yield

4 servings

Prep time

30 minutes

Cook time

15 to 20 minutes

2 tablespoons plus ½ teaspoon kosher salt, divided

1 pound elbow macaroni

6 tablespoons unsalted butter, divided

¼ cup flour

2 cups whole milk

4 cups shredded cheddar cheese

¼ teaspoon pepper

1 cup panko breadcrumbs

¼ cup grated Parmesan cheese

1. Bring a large pot of water to boil over high heat. Add 2 tablespoons of salt to the water.
2. Add the macaroni and cook according to the package directions.
3. Strain and set aside while making the sauce.
4. Heat a medium saucepan over low heat. Add 4 tablespoons of butter to the pan and melt.
5. Whisk the flour into the melted butter.
6. Cook the flour paste for 5 minutes, stirring constantly.
7. Slowly stream in the milk, whisking constantly. Increase the heat to medium to thicken.
8. Once the sauce is thick, add the cheese, ½ teaspoon of salt, and pepper.
9. Whisk to combine and reduce the heat to low.
10. Toss the pasta in the sauce to coat.
11. Preheat the oven to 400°F.
12. Melt the remaining 2 tablespoons of butter in a microwavable bowl.
13. Toss the breadcrumbs in the butter to coat.
14. Add the Parmesan cheese and mix to combine. Set aside.
15. Grease a 9 x 13-inch casserole dish.
16. Add the pasta mixture to the baking dish.
17. Top the pasta with an even layer of the breadcrumb mixture, making sure to sprinkle it into the corners and all the way out to the edges.
18. Bake for 15 to 20 minutes, until lightly golden brown on top.
19. Let cool for 5 minutes before serving warm.

Magic Star Fruit Salad

Let's make eating fruit more magical by mixing the fruit with a citrusy, sweet honey potion. This recipe works great as a side dish to any of the lunchtime dishes in this section, but you can also enjoy it as a snack.

Yield

6 servings

Cook time

20 minutes

¼ cup honey

2 tablespoons lemon juice

1 (15-ounce) can mandarin oranges, drained

2 cups strawberries, tops removed, hulled, and sliced

2 cups grapes, sliced in half

2 cups fresh pineapple chunks

1 cup blueberries

3 kiwis, peeled, sliced

1. In the base of a large bowl, whisk the honey and lemon juice to combine.
2. Toss all the fruit in the honey mixture.
3. Chill and serve cold.

Dinner

Burgers with Wizard Wizz-Bang Sauce

Burgers are a favorite of non-magical folk, and perhaps the house elves might have whipped up this dish for dinner as a treat for any homesick students. This take on the classic burger is a guaranteed crowd-pleaser, even for a burger-loving birthday boy who only got thirty-six presents this year (when last year he got thirty-seven).

Yield

4 burgers

Cook time

30 minutes

Wizard Wizz-Bang Sauce

½ cup mayonnaise

2 tablespoons ketchup

1 tablespoon yellow mustard

1 tablespoon chopped pickles

¼ teaspoon garlic powder

Burgers

1 pound ground beef

½ teaspoon garlic powder

½ teaspoon onion powder

¼ teaspoon paprika

1½ teaspoons kosher salt

½ teaspoon pepper

2 tablespoons canola oil

4 slices cheese

4 buns

4 leaves lettuce

1 large tomato, sliced

½ red onion, sliced (optional)

1. In a small bowl, mix all of the Wizard Wizz-Bang Sauce ingredients to combine.

2. Chill in the fridge until ready to use.

3. In a large bowl, combine the ground beef with the garlic powder, onion powder, paprika, salt, and pepper.

4. Divide the mixture into four and roll each portion into a ball.

5. Pat each ball into a ½-inch-thick, flat disc. Place on a plate and wash hands before moving on to the next step.

6. Heat the canola oil in a large skillet over medium heat. Gently place each burger into the pan.

7. Cook for 5 to 8 minutes on each side, until the burgers are browned and no pink remains.

8. Place one slice of cheese on top of each burger and allow to cook for an additional minute until the cheese melts.

9. Let the burgers rest while you prepare the buns.

10. Toast the buns, either in a toaster or in the same pan on medium-high heat, until lightly browned, 1 to 2 minutes.

11. Spread a dollop of the wizard sauce evenly on both sides of the buns.

12. To build the burgers, start by placing the lettuce on the bottom bun, followed by the burger patty, then the tomato and onion slices, if using, before finishing with the top bun.

Easy Chicken Pot Pie

Meat pies are a favorite at the castle, so this cookbook includes two. This one is a chicken pot pie that features the flavors of classic chicken noodle soup, all wrapped up in a flaky golden crust. It is inspired by the chicken and ham pies served at mealtimes.

Yield
4 servings

Cook time
45 minutes

Filling
4 tablespoons unsalted butter
½ large onion, diced
2 large carrots, diced
1 stalk celery, thinly sliced
2 cloves garlic, minced
4 tablespoons flour
1 cup chicken stock
¼ cup whole milk
½ pound cooked chicken, diced or shredded
1 cup frozen peas
1 teaspoon dried thyme
2 tablespoons chopped fresh parsley
½ teaspoon kosher salt
pepper, to taste

Crust
1 store-bought 9-inch pie dough
1 egg, beaten

1. Preheat the oven to 400°F.
2. Heat the butter in a medium saucepan over medium heat.
3. Add the onion, carrots, celery, and garlic. Sauté the vegetables until soft, about 10 minutes.
4. Add the flour to the pan and mix well. Cook for an additional 5 minutes.
5. Add the chicken stock and bring the mixture to a simmer.
6. Add the milk and chicken to the pan. Cook 2 to 3 minutes, until the chicken is warmed through.
7. Add the peas, thyme, parsley, salt, and pepper, and cook for another 2 minutes.
8. Remove the mixture from the heat and place in a large, round ovenproof baking dish.
9. Roll the pie dough out to slightly larger than the width of your baking dish on a lightly floured surface.
10. Place the dough on top of the filling, allowing the dough to drape over the sides of the dish by an inch. Trim any excess.
11. Make two slits in the dough at the center of the pot pie.
12. Brush the beaten egg all over the crust. Then bake the pie for 20 minutes until golden brown.
13. Allow the pie to rest 10 minutes before serving.

Shepherd's Pie

The second meat pie recipe is for shepherd's pie (also called a cottage pie), which is a very traditional English dish often served for dinner at the castle. Topped with mashed potatoes, this dish is the perfect way to fill up after a long day of classes.

Yield
4 servings

Cook time
1 hour

1 tablespoon olive oil
1 pound ground beef
2 teaspoons kosher salt, divided
½ large onion, diced
2 stalks celery, diced
2 large carrots, diced
1 clove garlic, minced
½ teaspoon black pepper
2 tablespoons tomato paste
1 tablespoon Worcestershire sauce
2 teaspoons chopped fresh rosemary, or 1 teaspoon dried
2 teaspoons fresh thyme, or 1 teaspoon dried
1 cup frozen peas
1 recipe Mashed Potatoes (page 72)

1. Preheat a broiler to high heat.
2. Heat the olive oil in a large skillet over medium heat.
3. Crumble the beef into the pan and season with 1 teaspoon of salt. Cook until browned and no pink remains.
4. Strain the beef onto a paper towel–lined plate, leaving about 1 tablespoon of fat in the pan.
5. Add the onion, celery, carrots, and garlic to the pan. Season with the remaining teaspoon of salt and the pepper. Sauté until soft, 8 to 10 minutes.
6. Add the tomato paste and cook for 2 minutes.
7. Add the Worcestershire sauce, rosemary, and thyme, and sauté another 2 minutes.
8. Add the frozen peas and remove the pan from the heat.
9. Pour the mixture into an 8 x 8-inch pan.
10. Spread the mashed potatoes evenly over the top.
11. Place the pie under the broiler and cook until golden brown on top, 3 to 5 minutes.
12. Let cool for 10 minutes before serving.

Mashed Potatoes and Gravy

Every great dinner needs some stellar side dishes, so it's no wonder that mashed potatoes are served at pretty much every castle dinner. This recipe is full of creamy, buttery goodness and is sure to please any witch, wizard, or nearly headless ghost at the dinner table. Paired with a rich gravy, you've got a crowd-pleasing side. Once you're comfortable with the gravy recipe, feel free to sprinkle the spices you prefer into your cauldron—this is a potion that benefits from experimentation (unlike the one that will turn you into a cat-human hybrid with just one wrong ingredient).

Yield
4 servings

Cook time
30 minutes

Gravy
4 tablespoons unsalted butter
¼ large onion, finely diced
2 cloves garlic, minced
4 tablespoons flour
1⅔ cups beef stock
1 teaspoon dried thyme
1 bay leaf
kosher salt and black pepper, to taste

Mashed Potatoes
2 pounds Yukon gold potatoes, peeled and cut into 1-inch chunks
4 tablespoons unsalted butter
2 teaspoons kosher salt
¼ cup whole milk

1. To make the gravy, melt the butter over medium heat in a medium saucepan.
2. Add the onion and garlic, sautéing 5 to 8 minutes until soft but not brown.
3. Add the flour and cook an additional 2 minutes until well incorporated with the butter in the pan.
4. Add the stock, thyme, and bay leaf.
5. Cook until thickened, about 5 minutes, whisking constantly to avoid the gravy sticking to the bottom of the pan.
6. Season with salt and pepper. Remove the bay leaf.
7. Leave on low heat while making the mashed potatoes.
8. Place the potatoes into a large pot of cold water and bring the pot to a boil over high heat.
9. Boil for 15 to 20 minutes until very tender; a fork should easily slide into a potato when tested.
10. Strain the potatoes and place them into the bowl of a stand mixer or into a large bowl if using a hand-held mixer.
11. Add the butter, salt, and milk. Whip until smooth and fluffy, 2 minutes on medium speed.
12. Serve the potatoes hot with gravy on top.

Bubble and Squeak

The castle loves to serve up a good potato dish at dinnertime, and bubble and squeak is a British classic. It's been around since at least the 1700s, so one can assume it's been a staple in the Great Hall for many, many years. I've simplified my flavor-packed bubble and squeak for kid chefs, but the dish still keeps its silly name.

Yield

4 servings

Cook time

30 minutes

20 baby Yukon gold potatoes

6 strips bacon or 8 sausage links, crumbled

¼ head green cabbage, roughly chopped

2 carrots, diced, or 1 cup green beans, cut in 1-inch pieces

¼ large onion, thinly sliced

1 teaspoon fresh thyme or ½ teaspoon dried

1 teaspoon chopped fresh rosemary, or ½ teaspoon dried

2 tablespoons unsalted butter, divided

2 tablespoons Worcestershire sauce

1 cup frozen peas

kosher salt and pepper, to taste

4 eggs

1. Fill a large pot with cold water.
2. Add the potatoes and bring to a boil over high heat.
3. Once boiling, cook the potatoes until tender, 10 to 15 minutes. To test tenderness, a fork should easily slide into a potato without much resistance.
4. Strain the potatoes and run cold water over them. Set aside and allow to cool.
5. Meanwhile, heat a medium sauté pan over medium heat.
6. Add the bacon strips or crumbled sausage to the pan and cook until done, 7 to 10 minutes.
7. Transfer the bacon or crumbled sausage to a paper towel–lined plate to cool.
8. In the same pan with the residual bacon fat, add the cabbage, carrots or green beans, and onion. Cook until they are soft, 7 to 10 minutes.
9. Next, quarter the potatoes and add them to the pan.
10. Roughly chop the bacon, if using. Return the bacon or sausage to the pan.
11. Add the thyme, rosemary, 1 tablespoon of butter, Worcestershire sauce, peas, salt, and pepper. Sauté for 1 to 2 minutes.
12. Heat another medium sauté pan over medium heat.
13. Add the remaining tablespoon of butter.
14. Crack the eggs into the pan and cook until the egg whites are set but the yolks are still slightly runny, 3 to 4 minutes.
15. Serve in a bowl with the potato mixture on the bottom and the egg on top or place the 4 eggs on the hash to serve family style.

Groundskeeper's Mystery Casserole

Who knows what our favorite half-giant's casserole was actually made of—last time I checked, cows don't have talons, they have hooves! This talonless recipe is hearty, filling, and perfect for a satisfying dinner on a brisk fall day.

Yield
6 servings

Cook time
1 hour

2 tablespoons plus 1 teaspoon kosher salt
1 (12-ounce) package wide egg noodles
2 tablespoons olive oil, divided
½ large onion, diced
2 stalks celery, thinly sliced
1 large carrot, diced
2 cloves garlic, minced
1 pound button mushrooms, thinly sliced
2 tablespoons chopped fresh parsley
½ teaspoon pepper
6 tablespoons unsalted butter, divided, plus more for greasing
4 tablespoons flour
2½ cups whole milk
¼ cup sour cream
1 pound cooked chicken, shredded or diced
½ cup bread crumbs
¼ cup shredded Parmesan cheese

1. Preheat the oven to 350°F and grease a 9 x 13-inch casserole pan with butter.
2. Bring a large pot of water to a boil. Add 2 tablespoons of salt.
3. Add the egg noodles and cook for 5 minutes. The noodles will not be completely cooked through, but that's okay.
4. Strain the noodles, toss with 1 tablespoon of olive oil, and set aside.
5. In a large sauté pan, heat the remaining tablespoon of olive oil over medium heat.
6. Add the onion, celery, carrot, and garlic to the pan.
7. Cook for 5 minutes, until the vegetables are just starting to soften.
8. Add the mushrooms to the pan and cook for an additional 5 minutes.
9. Add the parsley to the pan and season with the remaining salt and the pepper.
10. Remove from the heat and place the mixture in a bowl to cool.
11. Return the pan to the stove and over medium heat, melt 4 tablespoons of butter.
12. Once melted, whisk in the flour. This will create a thick paste. Cook this paste for 5 minutes, whisking constantly.
13. Slowly drizzle in the milk, whisking to avoid clumps. Continue to cook the sauce until thickened.
14. Whisk in the sour cream to combine, and remove from the heat.
15. Toss the noodles, chicken, and vegetable mixture in the sauce.
16. Add this mixture to the 9 x 13-inch pan.
17. Sprinkle the bread crumbs and Parmesan cheese over the top.

18. Dot the top of the casserole with small pieces of the remaining butter.

19. Bake for 20 to 25 minutes until the breadcrumbs are golden and the cheese is melted.

20. Let cool for 10 minutes before serving.

Vegetable Soup

Here's a recipe for warm, delicious vegetable soup. It's especially great for anyone with a runny nose or tummyache. Even if you're recovering from an eat slugs hex gone awry, this soup is sure to nourish and soothe.

Yield
6 servings

Cook time
45 minutes

2 tablespoons olive oil

½ large onion, diced

2 carrots, diced

1 celery stalk, diced

2 cloves garlic, minced

½ teaspoon kosher salt, plus more to taste

¼ teaspoon pepper, plus more to taste

3½ cups low-sodium vegetable stock

1 cup water

1 28-ounce can crushed tomatoes

1 teaspoon dried oregano

½ teaspoon dried thyme

1 cup mini pasta (such as mini farfalle or rotelli)

1 (15.5-ounce) cannellini beans, strained and rinsed

1 cup frozen cut green beans

1 cup frozen corn kernels

1 cup frozen peas

¼ cup fresh parsley, chopped

grated Parmesan, for serving (optional)

1. Heat a large pot over medium heat.
2. Add the olive oil to the pan.
3. Add the onion, carrots, celery, and garlic. Season with the salt and pepper.
4. Sauté for 7 to 8 minutes, until the vegetables are soft.
5. Next, add the stock, water, tomatoes, oregano, and thyme.
6. Increase the heat to medium-high and bring the mixture to a boil.
7. Once boiling, reduce the heat to low and simmer for 20 minutes.
8. Next, increase the heat back up to medium and add the pasta. Cook for another 10 to 12 minutes until the pasta is soft.
9. Add the cannellini beans, green beans, corn, peas, and parsley to the pot. Cook for another 2 to 3 minutes, just until the cannellini beans and frozen vegetables are heated through.
10. Taste the soup (be careful it will be hot!) and add more salt and pepper to taste.
11. Serve hot, topped with grated Parmesan, if using.

Chicken Fingers

Here's a meal for the picky eaters at any magical boarding school: crispy, yummy chicken fingers. Breading the chicken strips yourself adds an extra-special crunch, and pairing them with a homemade BBQ sauce inspired by the tureens of condiments served in the Great Hall makes this dish doubly delicious!

Yield
4 servings

Cook time
45 minutes

Chicken Fingers
2 cups panko bread crumbs
½ cup flour
¼ teaspoon black pepper
3 teaspoons kosher salt, divided
2 eggs
1 teaspoon garlic powder
1 teaspoon onion powder
½ teaspoon paprika
1 pound chicken tenders
canola oil, for drizzling

Easy BBQ sauce
½ cup ketchup
1 teaspoon Dijon mustard
1 teaspoon apple cider vinegar
1 tablespoon brown sugar
1 teaspoon onion powder
1 teaspoon garlic powder
½ teaspoon paprika

1. Preheat the oven to 425°F.
2. Place the panko bread crumbs on an aluminum foil–lined baking sheet, drizzle with canola oil, and toss to coat. Toast for 3 to 5 minutes in the oven until golden. Remove from the oven and set aside to cool.
3. Place the flour in a shallow bowl and mix with the black pepper and 1 teaspoon of salt.
4. Beat the eggs in another shallow bowl or pie plate.
5. Mix the cooled, toasted bread crumbs with the remaining salt, the garlic powder, onion powder, and paprika.
6. Dip the chicken tenders one at a time in the flour mixture to coat completely.
7. Next, place the chicken tenders in the egg mixture, again getting every bit of the chicken coated.
8. Lastly, place the chicken tenders in the bread crumbs, pressing the mixture into the chicken to make sure it sticks.
9. Place the chicken tenders on an aluminum-lined baking sheet (you can reuse the one from toasting the bread crumbs).
10. Drizzle the tenders lightly in oil and sprinkle with salt.
11. Bake for 16 minutes, until golden and opaque. They should register 165°F or above with a thermometer.
12. Make the BBQ sauce by combining all the ingredients for the sauce in a small saucepan.
13. Heat over medium heat until the brown sugar is melted and the sauce is hot, 5 minutes.
14. Serve the chicken fingers hot with BBQ sauce.

Fish and Chips

Fish and chips (a.k.a. fish and french fries) is a classic British dish. And while the Great Hall is certainly no corner chippy, one can assume the talented chefs in the kitchen have their own secret recipe for this traditional classic.

<u>Yield</u>
4 servings

<u>Cook time</u>
1 hour

<u>Fish</u>
1 pound white fish fillets deboned, skinless (such as cod, rockfish, or halibut), roughly cut into 4-inch portions
1 cup flour
2 eggs
2 tablespoons water
1½ cups panko bread crumbs
½ teaspoon dried thyme
¼ teaspoon paprika
1 teaspoon kosher salt
½ teaspoon pepper
canola oil, for drizzling

<u>Chips</u>
4 large Yukon gold potatoes, skin on, cut into 8 wedges each
2 tablespoons canola oil
1 teaspoon kosher salt
¼ teaspoon pepper
tartar sauce or ketchup to serve (optional)

1. Preheat the oven to 425°F, with one rack on the lower third of the oven and one on the upper third. Line a sheet pan with parchment paper.
2. Start with the chips, or fries. Toss the potatoes in the oil, salt, and pepper.
3. Scatter the potato wedges in a single layer onto the sheet pan.
4. Place in the oven on the upper rack and bake for 20 minutes.
5. To make the fish, line a sheet pan with parchment paper.
6. Next, create the breading station. Start by placing the flour on one plate.
7. In a large, flat bowl or pie plate, whisk the eggs with the water.
8. On a third plate, toss together the panko bread crumbs, thyme, paprika, salt, and pepper.
9. Dip the first piece of fish in the flour, then the egg mixture, followed by the panko. Make sure to coat every inch of the fish in each mixture and press the panko into the fish to adhere.
10. Place the piece of fish onto the sheet pan and continue the process until all the fish is coated. Drizzle each piece lightly with canola oil.
11. Using a spatula, flip each potato wedge over. Then rotate the potatoes to the bottom rack of the oven and place the breaded fish on the top rack to cook.
12. Cook for 10 to 15 minutes, until both the potatoes and fish are browned and crispy. The fish should register 145°F in the center when checked with a thermometer.
13. Serve warm with tartar sauce or ketchup, if using.

One Pan Chicken and Carrots

One pan dinners are so easy to make, it feels like magic! This recipe takes inspiration from the carrots that were served at the welcome feast, the end-of-term feast, and most likely many feasts in between.

<u>Yield</u>

4 servings

<u>Prep time</u>

5 minutes

<u>Cook time</u>

22 to 25 minutes

2 teaspoons fresh thyme or 1 teaspoon dried

2 tablespoons fresh chopped parsley or 1 tablespoon dried

1 teaspoon garlic powder

½ teaspoon onion powder

1 teaspoon pepper, divided

1 teaspoon kosher salt, divided

5 tablespoons extra-virgin olive oil, divided

4 boneless skinless chicken breasts, about 1½ pounds

1 pound carrots or vegetables of choice, sliced about 1/2-inch thick

1. Preheat the oven to 400°F.
2. Line a sheet pan with aluminum foil.
3. In a large bowl, combine the thyme, parsley, garlic powder, onion powder, ½ teaspoon of pepper, ½ teaspoon of salt, and 3 tablespoons of olive oil.
4. Add the chicken breasts to the bowl and toss with tongs or your hands to coat all of the chicken evenly in the oil mixture.
5. Place the chicken breasts on one half of the sheet pan. If you use your hands, wash them before going on to the next step!
6. In another medium bowl, combine the remaining olive oil, pepper, and salt.
7. Add the carrots to the bowl and toss to coat.
8. Add the carrots to the other half of the sheet pan.
9. Place in the oven and cook for 22 to 25 minutes, until the chicken is opaque and reads 165°F when inserted with a thermometer.
10. Allow chicken to rest for 5 minutes before serving alongside the carrots.

Dessert

Pumpkin Pasties

A magical must-have, pumpkin pasties are warm, packed with pumpkin flavor, and immensely satisfying. Plus, thanks to the fact that they're encased in a delicious golden crust, they are super portable. Perfect for a train ride, which is why they're offered on the trolley!

Yield

6 pasties

Prep and chill time

60 minutes

Cook time

30 minutes

Dough

2¼ cups flour, plus
more for dusting

½ teaspoon kosher salt

1½ tablespoons granulated sugar

1 cup (2 sticks) unsalted
butter, cubed, cold

⅓ cup ice water

Filling

1 cup pumpkin puree

5 tablespoons granulated sugar,
plus more for sprinkling

1 teaspoon ground cinnamon

pinch of kosher salt

1 egg

1. In a large mixing bowl whisk the flour, salt, and sugar together.
2. Add the cubed butter. Using your thumb and index fingers, pinch and rub the butter into roughly pea-sized pieces.
3. One tablespoon at a time, add the ice water, gently mixing with either a spatula or your hands.
4. Once all the water is added, the dough should loosely hold together and look shaggy. If the dough appears too dry, add one additional tablespoon of water at a time until it holds together.
5. Turn the dough out onto a lightly floured surface and pat into a flat disk. Wrap the dough in plastic and chill in the refrigerator for 30 minutes.
6. Preheat the oven to 400°F and line a cookie sheet with parchment paper.
7. While the dough chills, make the filling. In a small bowl, stir together the pumpkin puree, sugar, cinnamon, and salt.
8. In a separate small bowl, beat the egg and set aside.
9. Take the dough out of the fridge and divide it into six pieces.
10. Roll each piece into a ball. On a lightly floured surface using the palm of your hand, flatten each into a disc.
11. Working with one disc at a time, roll out each into a circle about ⅛-inch thick.
12. In the center of the first circle, place two tablespoons of the filling and fold the dough in half over the filling to form a half circle.
13. Seal the dough by firmly pressing all along the edges with a fork.
14. Repeat the process with the 5 remaining dough balls.
15. Place the pasties on the cookie sheet.

16. Brush each pasty with the beaten egg and then sprinkle each with sugar.
17. Using a paring knife, cut two slits in the top of each.
18. Bake for 15 minutes and then rotate the pan and bake for another 10 minutes until golden brown all over.
19. Let cool for at least 20 minutes before enjoying.

Cauldron Cakes

Here's a fun take on cauldron cakes, which are sold on the train trolley: a rich chocolate cake with a melty molten center. If you want to practice transfiguration, try to turn one of these cakes into a cabbage. Though be careful—that's a spell for sixth-years!

Yield
4 large or 6 small cakes

Cook time
30 minutes

nonstick cooking spray
2 tablespoons cocoa powder
5 ounces semisweet
chocolate, chopped
½ cup (1 stick) unsalted
butter, cubed
2 eggs
2 egg yolks
¼ cup granulated sugar
¼ teaspoon kosher salt
2 tablespoons flour
powdered sugar (optional)

1. Preheat the oven to 425°F. Grease 4, 6-ounce ramekins or 6 cups of a muffin tin with cooking spray.

2. Dust the ramekins or muffin tin with the cocoa powder, making sure there are no blank spots.

3. To a microwave-safe bowl, add the chocolate and butter.

4. Melt the chocolate and butter in 30-second increments, stirring the mixture between each increment. Set aside to cool to room temperature.

5. In the base of a stand mixer fitted with a whisk attachment or in a bowl with a whisk, whisk the eggs, egg yolks, sugar, and salt until pale and increased in volume.

6. Slowly whisk in the chocolate mixture to combine, then whisk in the flour.

7. Divide the batter among the 4 ramekins or 6 muffin cups, filling them three-quarters of the way up.

8. Bake for 12 to 14 minutes, until the edges of the cake look set and the center is puffed. If using a muffin tin, bake for only 8 to 10 minutes.

9. Allow to cool for 1 minute before having an adult help invert the warm cakes onto a plate. Dust the tops of cakes with powdered sugar, if using.

10. Serve warm, cracking open the center of the cakes to watch the little cauldrons ooze.

Treacle Tart

Treacle tart isn't just another English staple, it's also a certain dark-wizard defeating boy's favorite dessert. And who wouldn't love such a sweet treat? Made of only a few ingredients, it doesn't take much time or hassle to conjure up a simply splendid treacle tart.

Yield
8 servings

Cook time
1 hour

Shortbread Crust
½ cup (1 stick) unsalted butter
¼ cup powdered sugar
1 cup flour

Filling
1 tablespoon unsalted butter, melted
2 tablespoons whole milk
2 eggs
1 zested lemon
1 tablespoon lemon juice
½ cup molasses
1¼ cups fresh white breadcrumbs
whipped cream, to serve (optional)

1. Preheat the oven to 350°F.
2. In the bowl of a stand mixer fitted with a paddle attachment or with a hand-held mixer, cream the butter and sugar together until light and fluffy.
3. On low speed, slowly add in the flour until just combined.
4. Press the crust mixture evenly into a 9-inch tart pan with a removable bottom.
5. Using a fork, gently prick the crust all over.
6. Chill the crust for 15 minutes in the freezer.
7. Bake for 15 to 20 minutes until light brown.
8. Cool to room temperature.
9. To make the filling, in a large bowl, whisk together the melted butter, milk, eggs, lemon zest, lemon juice, and molasses to combine.
10. Fold in the bread crumbs until thoroughly coated.
11. Pour the mixture into the cooled crust and return to the oven for an additional 20 minutes.
12. Cool at least 20 minutes before topping with whipped cream, if using, and serving.

Easy Fudge

As part of his first-year Christmas haul, our protagonist got some delicious homemade fudge. Here is a recipe that is worthy of celebration at any time of the year.

Yield

12 servings

Cook time

10 minutes, plus 3 hours to set

nonstick cooking spray
3 tablespoons unsalted butter
1 (14-ounce) can sweetened condensed milk
2½ cups semisweet chocolate chips

1. Grease a bread pan with nonstick cooking spray. Line the pan with parchment paper, so that two flaps of paper hang over the sides of the pan.
2. In a medium saucepan, melt the butter over medium heat.
3. Add the sweetened condensed milk and chocolate chips.
4. Cook the mixture until smooth and all the chocolate chips are melted, stirring constantly.
5. Pour the mixture into the prepared pan, smoothing the top with the spatula.
6. Place the fudge in the fridge for at least 3 hours to set.
7. Once set, cut into 12 squares.
8. Store in an airtight container for up to a week.

Heart-Shaped Sugar Cookies

This classic sugar cookie recipe goes well with tea, coffee, or a glass of cold milk. While you're making these at home, be glad that you won't have to suffer through an awkward first date on Valentine's Day in order to enjoy them, although if you'd like to serve them up with some pink, heart confetti, that's up to you!

Yield
18 large cookies or
36 small cookies

Cook time
40 minutes, plus
30 minutes to chill

Dough
1 cup (2 sticks) unsalted butter, soft
½ cup granulated sugar
2 egg yolks
1 teaspoon vanilla extract
2 cups flour
½ teaspoon baking powder
¼ teaspoon kosher salt

Icing
1¾ cups powdered sugar
2 tablespoons light corn syrup
¼ cup whole milk
sprinkles

1. Start by creaming the butter and sugar on medium speed in the base of a stand mixer fitted with a paddle attachment or in a large bowl with a hand-held mixer.
2. When the butter mixture is light and fluffy, add the egg yolks, one at a time.
3. Once the egg yolks are completely incorporated, add the vanilla extract.
4. In a medium bowl, whisk together the flour, baking powder, and salt.
5. Slowly add the flour mixture into the butter mixture on low speed.
6. Mix until just incorporated; overmixing will make the cookies tough.
7. Transfer the dough onto a clean surface and flatten it into a disk.
8. Wrap the dough in plastic and chill in the fridge for 30 minutes.
9. Preheat the oven to 350°F.
10. Once chilled, roll out the dough to ¼-inch thickness on a lightly floured surface with a lightly floured rolling pin.
11. Use the cookie cutter to cut out hearts. Try to keep as little space between each cut as possible and dip the cutter in flour every few cuts to avoid sticking.
12. Place the cookies 1 inch apart on an ungreased cookie sheet.
13. Gather the dough scraps and roll the dough out once more, up to three times total, to cut out more hearts. Discard any leftover dough.

14. Chill the cookies in the fridge for 10 minutes.

15. Bake for 14 minutes, rotating halfway through. The cookies should be a light color and just set. Too much browning will make them hard.

16. Allow the cookies to cool on the cookie sheets for 5 minutes before placing them on a cooling rack to cool completely.

17. Make the icing. In a medium bowl, combine the powdered sugar, corn syrup, and milk.

18. Whisk until the mixture is combined and smooth.

19. When the cookies are completely cooled, place a small dollop of icing, about the size of a quarter, in the center of the cookie.

20. Using a butter knife or an offset spatula, spread the icing evenly over the cookie just up to the edge but not over.

21. Add the sprinkles and then allow the cookie to dry on a plate or cooling rack until the icing hardens, 20 minutes.

22. Store in an airtight container for up to 5 days.

Fizzy Whizbees

Though this version of the popular wizarding candy won't actually make you float, it will make you feel like you could! This is a guaranteed party in your mouth thanks to the sour citric acid and the pop rocks.

Yield

5 dozen candies

Prep time

30 minutes, plus 2 hours to dry

1¼-ounce packet
unflavored gelatin

1 tablespoon lemon juice

1 tablespoon lime juice

2 tablespoons water,
room temperature

1 (2-pound) bag powdered sugar

1 tablespoon instant
lemonade powder

¾ teaspoon citric acid

food coloring of choice

Pop Rocks, crushed

cornstarch, for dusting

1. In a microwave-safe bowl, combine the gelatin, lemon juice, lime juice, and water. Let the mixture sit for 2 minutes.

2. Microwave the mixture in 30-second increments, stirring in between each increment, until the gelatin is completely dissolved.

3. Add the mixture to the bowl of a stand mixer fitted with a paddle attachment and add ¼ of the bag of powdered sugar. Mix to combine.

4. Add another ¼ of the powdered sugar into the bowl, mix completely, and repeat until all the sugar is incorporated.

5. Add the lemonade powder and citric acid. Mix well to combine.

6. Remove the mixture from the mixer and use a rubber spatula to slowly fold in the food coloring until the desired color is achieved. (Alternately, divide the mixture into multiple bowls and dye each a different color.)

7. To a small bowl, add the Pop Rocks.

8. Dust your hands with cornstarch and grab marble-sized pieces of the dough.

9. Roll the dough into balls, then roll the balls in the Pop Rocks to coat.

10. Dry the balls on a baking sheet lined with parchment paper for 2 hours before enjoying.

Birthday Cake Pops

In honor of our bespectacled protagonist's birthday, these cake pops are inspired by the shape and color of the enchanted golden ball he seeks during sports games, but feel free to adjust the color and decorations to your own taste!

<u>Yield</u>

24 cake pops

<u>Cook time</u>

2 hours

<u>Cake</u>

½ cup (1 stick) unsalted butter, soft

1 cup granulated sugar

2 eggs, room temperature

1 teaspoon vanilla extract

1½ cups flour

1½ teaspoons baking powder

¼ teaspoon kosher salt

½ cup whole milk

<u>Buttercream Frosting</u>

½ cup (1 stick) unsalted butter, soft

2 cups powdered sugar, sifted

1 teaspoon whole milk

½ teaspoon vanilla extract

1. Preheat the oven to 350°F. Grease and line one 9-inch cake pan with parchment.

2. Make the cake. In the bowl of a stand mixer fitted with a paddle attachment or in a large bowl with a hand-held mixer, beat the butter and sugar until light and fluffy, 2 to 3 minutes.

3. Add the eggs, one at a time, scraping the bowl down between additions.

4. Add the vanilla extract to the bowl, mixing well to combine.

5. In a medium bowl, sift together the flour, baking powder, and salt.

6. Alternate adding the flour mixture and the milk until both are completely mixed into the batter, scraping down the bowl in between additions of each.

7. Add the batter to the prepared pan, smoothing the top to make it level. Bake for 25 to 30 minutes until golden brown and a toothpick inserted in the center comes out clean.

8. Allow the cake to cool in the pan for 15 to 20 minutes before inverting it onto a cooling rack to finish cooling to room temperature.

9. Make the frosting. In the bowl of a stand mixer or in a large bowl with a hand mixer, beat the butter until it is light and fluffy, 2 to 3 minutes.

10. Slowly add the powdered sugar on low speed. Mix until combined, scraping down the bowl halfway through to ensure all the sugar gets incorporated, 5 minutes.

11. Add the milk and vanilla extract. Mix on low until just combined.

To Decorate

4 cups white candy melts

24 lollipop sticks

2 empty egg cartons

sprinkles (optional)

1 can gold color shimmer food spray; other metallic colors optional

12. To assemble, crumble the cooled cake into a large bowl.

13. Add the buttercream to the bowl. Using a spatula, mix the cake and buttercream frosting together until it forms a smooth dough-like mixture.

14. Roll the mixture into 24 even balls, using about 1 rounded tablespoon of mixture per ball.

15. Chill the balls in the refrigerator on a cookie sheet lined with parchment paper, 5 to 10 minutes.

16. Meanwhile, melt the candy melts for the decoration in a medium microwave-safe bowl, heating them in 30-second increments and stirring between increments.

17. Prepare the drying rack next. Invert two empty egg cartons. Poke each egg cup with the lollipop sticks. Set aside.

18. Remove the cake balls from the fridge. Dip each lollipop stick in the candy melt mixture and then poke it into a cake ball. This will help keep them on the stick when dipping later. Let them dry until hard on the parchment-lined cookie sheet.

19. Dip an entire cake pop into the candy melt mixture. If needed, spoon the mixture over the ball to coat it evenly.

20. Place the cake pop in the egg carton drying rack. Add sprinkles, if using, on top before the cake pop dries. Repeat with the remaining cake pops.

21. Allow 5 to 10 minutes for the cake pops to dry completely before spraying them with golden food spray.

22. Let the spray dry for 5 minutes, then enjoy!

Homemade Strawberry Ice Cream

This recipe is inspired by what our favorite trio has for dessert the night before the infamous world cup game. Don't be afraid to make your own ice cream at home. This recipe is easy to nail, and once you get the hang of it, you can experiment with different flavors for future batches.

Yield
12 servings

Prep time
20 minutes, plus 2 hours to freeze and 12 hours to set

2 cups strawberries, diced, divided

2 cups heavy whipping cream

1 (14-ounce) can sweetened condensed milk

1 teaspoon vanilla extract

¼ teaspoon kosher salt

1. Begin by pureeing 1 cup of strawberries in a blender.
2. In the bowl of a stand mixer fitted with a whisk attachment, add the heavy whipping cream. Whip on high speed until stiff peaks form; the cream should stand firmly on the whisk attachment when dipped and removed from the bowl.
3. In another large bowl, stir together the pureed strawberries, sweetened condensed milk, vanilla extract, and salt.
4. Using a spatula, gently fold in the whipped cream until no streaks of white remain.
5. Pour the mixture into a bread pan and freeze for 2 hours.
6. Swirl in the remaining 1 cup of strawberry pieces and return to the freezer to set overnight.

Knickerbocker Glory

The knickerbocker glory is an ice cream extravaganza with layers of ice cream, fruit, sauce, and whatever else you'd like. This dessert is perfect for any birthday or special occasion, thanks to the magical homemade strawberry sauce, though you might need a stomach-expanding charm to be able to finish the whole bowl!

<u>Yield</u>
4 sundaes

<u>Cook time</u>
20 minutes

<u>Strawberry Sauce</u>
1 cup strawberries, tops removed, hulled, and sliced
½ cup granulated sugar
1 tablespoon lemon juice

<u>Sundaes</u>
12 scoops vanilla ice cream
12 crushed vanilla wafer cookies
1 pint blueberries or strawberries, sliced
whipped cream, to serve
8 pirouette cookies, to serve (optional)
4 maraschino cherries

1. In a small saucepan, combine all of the ingredients for the sauce. Bring them to a boil over high heat and then reduce the heat to low.

2. Cook the mixture until the strawberries have reached a syrupy consistency, 5 minutes.

3. Allow the sauce to cool to room temperature before using.

4. To assemble your sundaes, place one scoop of ice cream in the bottom of four tall glasses.

5. Drizzle with the strawberry sauce, then sprinkle with the crushed wafer cookies, and top with a few blueberries or sliced strawberries.

6. Repeat the process twice more until each glass has three scoops of ice cream.

7. Top each glass with whipped cream, 2 pirouette cookies (if using), and a cherry.

Acid Lollipops

Inspired by the candy sold in the village by the castle, these pops can be as sour as you'd like, thanks to the citric acid. Just be sure you don't burn a hole through your tongue like our redhead best friend did!

Yield
12

Prep time
10 minutes, plus 30 minutes to dry

12 lollipops, any shape or flavor
½ cup light corn syrup or honey
1 tablespoon citric acid
4 tablespoons granulated sugar
empty egg carton

1. Start by unwrapping all the lollipops. Use the stick of the lollipops to poke holes in the bottom of an empty egg carton; this will be your drying rack.
2. In a small bowl, place the corn syrup or honey.
3. In another small bowl, stir together the citric acid and sugar.
4. Dip a lollipop into the corn syrup or honey, tapping off any excess to leave a thin coat.
5. Next, dip the lollipop into the sugar mixture to coat.
6. Place the lollipop into one of the holes in the inverted egg carton, to dry.
7. Repeat steps 4 to 6 with the rest of the lollipops.
8. Allow the acid pops to dry for 30 minutes, and they are ready to eat.

Sticky Toffee Pudding

This recipe is inspired by the dessert served at the entrance to the magical shopping alley in London. Full of warm, sugary goodness, this pudding is excellent on its own but even better with a homemade sauce.

Yield

12 servings

Prep time

30 minutes

Cook time

35 to 40 minutes

Cake

1 cup plus 1 tablespoon unsalted butter, soft, divided

36 pitted Medjool dates

2 cups boiling hot water

1 tablespoon plus 1 teaspoon instant espresso

1 teaspoon vanilla extract

1½ cups granulated sugar

5 eggs, room temperature

3 cups flour

1½ teaspoons baking powder

1 teaspoon kosher salt

1. Preheat the oven to 350°F. Grease a 9 x 13-inch pan with 1 tablespoon of butter, coating every inch of the pan.

2. Make the cake. Place the dates in a large bowl, pour the boiling hot water over them, and let sit until the water is cool enough to touch.

3. Add the espresso powder into the date mixture and stir to dissolve.

4. Blend the mixture, water and all, in a blender or food processor until the dates are broken into small pieces.

5. Stir in the vanilla extract and set aside.

6. In the bowl of a stand mixer fitted with a paddle attachment or with a handheld mixer, cream 1 cup of butter with the sugar until light and fluffy.

7. Slowly mix in one egg at a time, scraping down the bowl after adding each one.

8. In a medium bowl, whisk together the flour, baking powder, and salt.

9. Add one-third of the flour mixture to the butter mixture and mix on low speed to incorporate.

10. Add half of the reserved date mixture and mix on low speed, scraping down the bowl after mixing.

11. Add another third of the flour mixture, then add the rest of the date mixture.

12. Scrape down the bowl again and add the remaining flour mixture, mixing until just incorporated.

13. Scrape the batter into the prepared pan and bake for 35 to 40 minutes, until a toothpick inserted in the center comes out clean.

Sauce

½ cup (1 stick) unsalted butter

½ cup granulated sugar

¼ teaspoon kosher salt

½ cup heavy whipping cream

¼ cup pecan pieces

whipped cream, to
serve (optional)

orange zest, to serve (optional)

14. Allow the cake to cool and prepare the sauce. In a medium saucepan, melt the butter over low heat.

15. Once melted, add the sugar and salt. Increase the heat to medium high.

16. Cook this mixture, stirring constantly until it turns a deep brown color, about 15 minutes.

17. Add the heavy whipping cream and continue to cook for another minute.

18. Stir in the pecans and remove the sauce from the heat. Let cool for 15 minutes.

19. Once cooled, cut a square of the cake from the pan and drizzle the syrup over it. Top with whipped cream and orange zest, if using, and serve warm.

Self-Propelling Custard Pie

This recipe is a nod to our favorite twins and their hilarious wizarding joke shop. Feel free to enchant your pie to be self-propelling once it's done cooling, or simply eat it. After all, it's delicious!

Yield

1 (9-inch) pie

Prep time

1 hour

Cook Time

45 to 55 minutes, plus
4 hours to set

Custard

5 eggs, divided
¾ cup granulated sugar
1 cup whole milk
1 cup buttermilk
1 teaspoon vanilla extract
¼ teaspoon kosher salt

Crust

1 batch dough from
Pumpkin Pasties (page 88),
or 1 store-bought pie crust
whipped cream, to
serve (optional)

1. Preheat the oven to 400°F.
2. Take the dough out of the fridge and roll to ⅛-inch thickness on a lightly floured surface.
3. Carefully place the dough inside a 9-inch pie pan. An inch of dough should hang over the edge of the pan. Tuck the overhanging dough inside the lip of the pie pan to form an edge. Using your thumb and index finger, pinch the edge of the dough into a crimp.
4. Chill the crust for 15 minutes in the freezer.
5. Remove the crust from the freezer and line it with parchment paper and pie weights. Bake for 25 minutes.
6. Remove the pie weights from the crust and bake an additional 5 to 10 minutes, until the bottom of the crust is lightly brown. If the dough puffs slightly, push it down using the bottom of a measuring cup to flatten.
7. Lower the oven temperature to 350°F.
8. Next, make the custard. To a large bowl, add 3 whole eggs and 2 egg yolks. Reserve the 2 egg whites.
9. Whisk in the sugar, milk, buttermilk, vanilla, and salt until completely combined.
10. Brush the pie crust with a thin layer of egg white and return to the oven for 1 to 2 minutes until the egg white is dry; this will help to keep the crust from getting soggy.
11. Place the pie shell on a sheet pan, then fill it with the custard. Carefully transfer to the oven.
12. Bake for 45 to 55 minutes. The custard should have puffed up and will jiggle slightly when moved, but shouldn't wobble excessively.
13. Allow the pie to cool on a cooling rack until it reaches room temperature, then refrigerate it for at least 4 hours to set. Serve it cold with whipped cream, if using.

Drinks

Butterscotch "Beer"

A wizarding world favorite, this "beer" recipe allows you to enjoy a cup full of butterscotch-y goodness whenever you'd like, even if you aren't at a wizarding bar.

Yield
4 glasses

Cook time
25 minutes

½ cup (1 stick) butter
1 cup brown sugar
1 teaspoon kosher salt
2 teaspoons vanilla extract
1 cup heavy whipping cream
20 ounces lemon-lime soda
ice

1. In a medium saucepan over medium-low heat, melt the butter.
2. When the butter is melted, add the brown sugar, salt, and vanilla extract. Whisk to combine.
3. Cook the mixture for 5 minutes, until the brown sugar is completely dissolved.
4. Whisk in the heavy whipping cream and continue to cook for 1 minute.
5. Allow this mixture to cool to room temperature, 15 minutes.
6. When cool, divide between 4 large glasses filled halfway up with ice.
7. Slowly top with soda, but be careful not to overfill, as the mixture will bubble and foam! Stir to blend and enjoy.

Pumpkin Juice

A beloved classic, pumpkin juice is served with nearly every meal at the castle, as well as on the scarlet steam engine. This recipe is best served very cold or over ice.

Yield
2 servings

Cook time
10 minutes, plus 1 hour to chill

½ cup pumpkin puree
2 cups apple juice
2 tablespoons brown sugar
½ teaspoon ginger
½ teaspoon ground cinnamon

1. Start by whisking all the ingredients together in a medium saucepan.
2. Place the pan over medium heat and bring to a simmer.
3. Cook for 1 to 2 minutes, just until the brown sugar is dissolved.
4. Remove from the heat and allow to cool to room temperature.
5. Place the mixture into a pitcher to chill until cold, 1 hour.
6. Pour over ice, if desired, and enjoy!

Charming Cherry Soda

This recipe is inspired by the charms professor's favorite drink. For an authentic and festive finish, add an umbrella.

<u>Yield</u>

2 servings

<u>Cook time</u>

5 minutes

¼ cup granulated sugar

¼ water

1 cup unsweetened cherry juice

1 cup seltzer

ice

maraschino cherries,
to serve (optional)

1. In a small saucepan, combine the sugar and water.
2. Heat the mixture over medium heat, until the sugar melts and the mixture turns clear.
3. Set aside and allow to cool.
4. Fill two glasses up halfway with ice.
5. Divide the cherry juice between the two glasses.
6. Add 2 tablespoons of the sugar syrup to each glass.
7. Top each glass with a ½ cup of seltzer.
8. If using, add in a maraschino cherry or two.
9. Stir to blend, and enjoy.

Hot Chocolate with Whipped Cream

There's nothing more comforting than curling up with a cup of rich hot chocolate on a cold winter's day. Try adding a variety of toppings, like marshmallows or sprinkles, to make your mug even more magical. If you aren't in the mood to make your own whipped cream, feel free to conjure up a can of Reddi-wip!

Yield

4 servings

Cook time

10 minutes

Hot Chocolate

¼ cup cocoa powder

½ cup granulated sugar

pinch of kosher salt

1 teaspoon vanilla extract

4 cups whole milk

Whipped Cream

1 cup heavy whipping cream, cold

1 tablespoon powdered sugar

½ teaspoon vanilla extract

1. Using a whisk, combine the cocoa powder, sugar, and salt in a medium saucepan.
2. Whisk the vanilla extract and milk into the cocoa mixture.
3. Bring the mixture to a simmer over medium-low heat, whisking frequently to make sure the cocoa mixture incorporates and doesn't stick to the bottom of the pan.
4. Once the mixture is warm, 5 to 8 minutes, remove it from the heat and divide it between 4 mugs.
5. Make the whipped cream. Add the cold whipping cream to the bowl of a stand mixer fitted with a whisk attachment or to a large bowl with a handheld mixer, and begin to whip at medium speed.
6. Once the mixture has thickened slightly, add the sugar and vanilla extract.
7. Increase the mixer speed to medium-high. Whip until the cream is thick and fluffy. Be careful not to overwhip, as the cream will become lumpy. To check if the cream is ready, detach the whisk attachment or a mixer beater and see if the cream on the end forms a peak; if it does, it's ready! If not, continue to whip for a minute more at a time until it does.
8. Top each mug of hot chocolate with a dollop of whipped cream. Serve hot.

Orange Juice

If pumpkin juice isn't your thing, you'll no doubt enjoy this easy peasy recipe for freshly squeezed orange juice. This drink is served at breakfast in the Great Hall, but it also serves as a great pick-me-up in between classes.

Yield

2 servings

Prep time

5 minutes, plus 1 hour to chill

8 oranges, sliced in half

1. Set a fine-mesh strainer over a large bowl.
2. Squeeze the oranges halves over the strainer to catch the seeds and pulp.
3. Place the strained juice in a large pitcher and chill for an hour until cold.

FUN VARIATION

Substitute 4 oranges with ½ cup of mango juice and ½ cup of pineapple juice for a tropical orange juice drink.

Conversions

Volume

U.S.	U.S. Equivalent	Metric
1 tablespoon (3 teaspoons)	½ fluid ounce	15 milliliters
¼ cup	2 fluid ounces	60 milliliters
⅓ cup	3 fluid ounces	80 milliliters
½ cup	4 fluid ounces	120 milliliters
⅔ cup	5 fluid ounces	160 milliliters
¾ cup	6 fluid ounces	180 milliliters
1 cup	8 fluid ounces	240 milliliters
2 cups	16 fluid ounces	480 milliliters

Weight

U.S.	Metric
½ ounce	15 grams
1 ounce	30 grams
2 ounces	60 grams
¼ pound	115 grams
⅓ pound	150 grams
½ pound	225 grams
¾ pound	340 grams
1 pound	450 grams

Temperature

Fahrenheit (°F)	Celsius (°C)
70°F	20°C
100°F	40°C
120°F	50°C
130°F	55°C
140°F	60°C
150°F	65°C
160°F	70°C
170°F	75°C
180°F	80°C
190°F	90°C
200°F	95°C
220°F	105°C

Fahrenheit (°F)	Celsius (°C)
240°F	115°C
260°F	125°C
280°F	140°C
300°F	150°C
325°F	165°C
350°F	175°C
375°F	190°C
400°F	200°C
425°F	220°C
450°F	230°C
500°F	260°C

About the Author

Alana Al-Hatlani is a baker by morning and food writer by night. Her writing has appeared in *Saveur*, *Eater*, the *Seattle Times*, the *Seattle Weekly*, and the *Independent*. She is a cake-stand collector, a very competitive bowler, and *Great British Bake-Off* zealot. She started baking as soon as she could reach the counter with a step stool and hasn't left the kitchen since.

Alana holds a BA in journalism from New York University and a pastry degree from the Seattle Culinary Academy. To see more of her baking or writing, visit www.alanaalhatlani.com.